Make your own Rag Doll

Alicia Merrett

RUNNING PRESS
PHILADELPHIA · LONDON

A QUARTO BOOK

Library of Congress Cataloging-in-Publication Number 94-74314
ISBN 1-56138-618-9

This book was designed and produced by
Quarto Publishing plc, The Old Brewery, 6 Blundell Street, London N7 9BH

Senior Editor Laura Washburn • **Copy Editor** Cathy Meeus • **Art Editor** Julie Francis • **Designer** Debbie Mole • **Illustrator** Vana Haggerty • **Photographers** Paul Forrester and Laura Wickenden • **Art Director** Moira Clinch • **Editorial Director** Mark Dartford

Typeset by Central Southern Typesetters, Eastbourne
Manufactured in Hong Kong by Regent Publishing Services Ltd.
Printed and components supplied by Sing Cheong Printing Co Ltd, Hong Kong.
This book may be ordered by mail from the publisher.
Please include $2.50 for postage and handling. *But try your bookstore first!*
Running Press Book Publishers
125 South Twenty-second Street
Philadelphia, Pennsylvania 19103-4399

Quarto would like to thank the following who provided dolls or doll designs for the gallery:
Crafts Beautiful magazine, Faith Eaton,
Hinsdale Antiques, Sally Lampi, Alicia Merrett, Fadila Skalli.

A Note to Parents
This kit is not designed for young children. It contains small parts that could cause injury, including severe injury if swallowed. This kit should not be used by children without adult supervision.

Contents

Introduction

Rag dolls have existed since the earliest times. Traditionally, they are made from materials that are easy to find in and around the home: scraps of fabric, old stockings, left-over knitting yarn, straw, rugs, buttons, and so on. Stuffings include sawdust, straw, rags, wool, and kapok.

Throughout their history, rag dolls have been fashioned not only by people in their homes, but also by artists and craft-workers. They have been made for adults as well as for children. Their simplicity, softness, and friendly expressions endear them to everybody.

Rag dolls come in all shapes, sizes, textures, and degrees of firmness. Faces can be flat or may give a more three-dimensional impression. The features can be simply drawn in ink or paint or they can be more elaborately sewn, using appliqué or embroidery. The doll in the kit provided is of a traditional type, with calico body, embroidered features, yarn hair, lace-edged under-wear, print dress, and boots. The face has a short seam to form a slightly shaped nose. She has her own tiny rag dolly that fits into the pocket of her dress.

There are sufficient materials in the kit to enable you to complete one doll, but you can make many others using the same pattern and following our instructions for alternative faces, hairstyles, clothes, and accessories. Cut the "hair" short for a boy doll. Choose a different color body fabric to make a non-Caucasian doll. Use other types of yarn to create different hair textures. There are instructions for making a flatter face, and for how to paint the face instead of embroidering it. The doll's limbs can be jointed with buttons instead of stitched, which creates a more sophisticated toy for an older child or adult.

You can make larger or smaller dolls by using a photocopier to increase or reduce the size of the patterns. In this way you can give your original doll younger or older brothers and sisters. There are also instructions for making accessories for your dolls. In this way, you can be sure that every doll you make is truly individual.

Tools and equipment

Your sewing basket, stationery drawer, and remnants' box should contain most of the tools needed to make a rag doll.

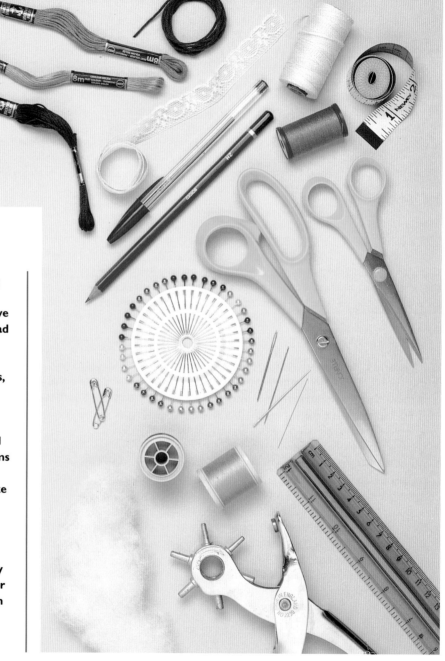

Needles for hand stitching: Use sharp sewing needles for seams. For embroidery, crewel embroidery needles are preferable – they have large eyes, which make the embroidery thread easier to handle.

Pins: Choose stainless steel dressmaker's pins, either plain or with glass heads.

Sewing machine: Although all parts of a rag doll can be stitched by hand, for strength and safety, it is recommended that the main seams are stitched by machine. Fit a No. 11 or 14 needle in your machine, and set the stitch size to 2½ for straight stitching, and No. 4 for the gathering rows.

Scissors: For cutting fabric, use sharp dressmaking shears. Fine-pointed embroidery scissors are best for snipping curves and other small jobs. All-purpose household scissors can be used for cutting paper.

Threader or safety pin: You will need this to thread elastic through casings.

Tape measure and a ruler: Accurate measurements and a straight edge or ruler are needed to draw the patterns for some of the dress pieces.

Pencil and ballpoint pen: These are used for tracing the patterns and marking them on the fabrics.

Sewing thread: General purpose, cotton, or polyester thread should be used for normal machine or hand stitching.

Extra strong (button) thread: This is needed only if you are making a jointed doll.

Embroidery thread: Choose stranded cotton embroidery thread for the features.

Fillings: Polyester is best.

Lace: This is needed for edging the underwear.

Fine cord or thick embroidery thread: This is used for the doll's boot laces.

Leather punch: This is useful for making the tiny holes in the boots for the laces.

Yarn: You can use many different types for the hair, including wool and acrylic. The choice is determined by the effect you want (see Making dolls' hair, page 8).

Ribbons: These are used for making optional decorations for the hair and dress.

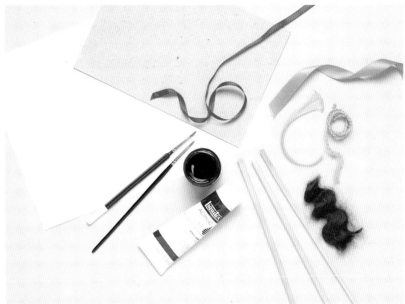

Paper: Ordinary typing paper is good for copying patterns onto. You will also need some scrap paper for preparing the hair sections.

Stuffing tools: To press the stuffing into the ends of the fingers and toes, you will need either a medium-to-thick knitting needle or a tapered dowel (a chopstick is ideal). Alternatively, use the end of a fine paintbrush.

Thin cardboard: This is used for reinforcing paper patterns that you may wish to re-use. You will also need some cardboard around which to wind the yarn when making the hair sections.

Paints: You will need these if you choose to make the alternative painted face. Acrylic or fabric paints are best. These should be applied with a fine brush. Fine fabric markers or drawing pens filled with permanent brown or black ink are useful for fine lines.

Fabrics and stitches

Fabrics

In the kit you have all the fabric you need for your first doll. For additional dolls you will need to buy additional materials. On this page you will find some suggestions for suitable fabrics. Only a few simple stitches are needed for sewing your rag doll. On the facing page, instructions are given for all the stitches you will need. Stem stitch and satin stitch are used for embroidering the doll's features.

Muslin: (preferably unbleached) is a strong, all-purpose fabric for the doll body, but other firm, woven cottons can be used.

Fine cotton batiste, or cotton polyester: These fabrics are good for underwear, nightwear, and fine blouses or shirts.

Cotton or cotton polyester prints: A pretty print in one of these fabrics is usually the first choice for dresses.

Plain-colored cotton: Heavy cotton is best for trousers and jackets.

Stretch cotton: T-shirts and sweatshirts can be made from this type of fabric for a doll with a more modern look.

Imitation suede: This is excellent for boots and shoes.

Felt: This is a good alternative for boots and shoes, but needs to be reinforced with an iron-on backing material. Felt is also useful for a variety of other accessories.

Stitches

Backstitch: This is for stitching body and clothes by hand. Bring the thread through on the stitch line, then take a small stitch backward to the right. Bring the needle back to the front, a little in front of the previous stitch. Continue along the sewing line.

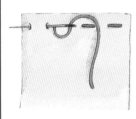

Gathering stitch: This is a large running stitch that allows you to pull the thread to gather the waist and ruffle of the dress.
By hand – Thread the needle with doubled thread longer than the line to be stitched. Make medium-size running stitches along the line. Run a second gathering line ⅛in below the first, for strength. Pull the ends of the threads from the two lines of stitching together to form the gathers.
By machine – Set the stitch length to No. 4. Run two rows as indicated above, and then pull the two lower threads evenly to gather.

Basting: Use these large running stitches to hold layers of fabric in place temporarily. They can be easily removed after the final stitching.

Stab stitch: This is a running stitch in which you pull the thread fully through the fabric after each stitch. It is used for stitching through thick layers of fabric and/or stuffing.

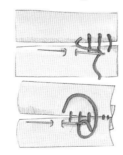

Ladder stitch: This is an invisible stitch that is mainly used for closing openings. It is similar to a running stitch, but each stitch is taken on alternate sides of the seam. Pull the thread tight every few stitches to close the seam.

Hem stitch: Use this stitch for finishing hems, cuffs, collar bindings, etc. With the hem pinned or basted in place, bring the thread through the hem fold onto the wrong side. Take a tiny diagonal stitch, first on the main fabric and then on the hem fold. Pull through and repeat, keeping the stitches small and close together.

Satin stitch: This is used for the eyes and mouth. Work straight stitches closely together across the required shape to produce a solid area of color.

Stem stitch: This outline stitch is used for eyebrows, eyelids, and other lines on the face. Work from left to right, taking small regular stitches along the line of the design. Always bring the thread out on the left side of the previous stitch.

Making dolls' hair

Traditionally rag dolls have hair made from knitting yarn. There are many types of yarns, most of which are suitable for making dolls' hair. There are smooth yarns and fuzzy yarns, fine yarns and thick yarns. Thick yarns can be unraveled to separate out their component strands, producing the impression of curly hair. Other materials often make effective alternatives to yarn – for example, linen, raffia, knitting ribbon, cut or torn strips of fabric, braided crepe wool, theatrical mohair, unspun wool.

Long hair

For a simple, traditional long hairstyle, you need sufficient length of wool to allow for braiding or "ponytails," and sufficient width to cover the doll's head from the top of the forehead to the back of the neck. You can calculate the amount required by taking two basic measurements:

Length – Measure the finished length required from the top of the doll's head. Double this amount and add an extra 1/4in to allow for the amount to be taken up by braiding. In this example the length measurement is 20in.

Width – Measure from the top of the forehead (which is a little bit in front of the seam line at the top of the head), over the top of the head, down to the beginning of the back neck. For a doll made to the standard pattern size the width measurement is 4¼in.

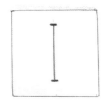

1 Mark the width measurement with a pencil line in the middle of a piece of scrap paper.

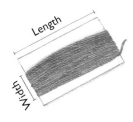

2 Wind the wool around cardboard that has been cut to the required measurement for the length. When the width of the wound wool matches the width measurement, carefully remove it from the carboard.

3 Place the wool over the prepared piece of paper, with the lengthwise center lying on the marked line. Fit the width onto the line, too.

4 Machine stitch the yarn onto the paper, going over it twice. Tear off the paper.

5 Stitch the "hair" to the doll's head along the stitched line, to make a center parting. Cut the loops at the ends and comb through with your fingers. Trim as necessary to make sure of an even length.

6 Braid or gather the hair in "bunches" with a ribbon. It is advisable to secure the hair to the side neck with a few back stitches hidden in the strands of yarn. Other hairstyles may require stitching at different points along the hair length.

Short hair

This style is appropriate if you are making a boy doll. It can also be used for girl dolls with short hair and, if made with a curly or fuzzy wool, it makes an excellent African hairstyle. The basic procedure consists of preparing long "bangs" of wound wool that are then attached to the head in a spiral fashion.

1 Fold some scrap paper to a width of 3in. Prepare enough pieces of folded paper to make a total length of 30in. The paper does not need to be all in one piece. The yarn can be wound up in different widths, to produce longer or shorter hairstyles.

2 Wind the yarn onto the paper pieces, until the whole length is covered.

3 Machine stitch lengthwise along the center of the yarn and paper, as for long hair.

4 Tear off the paper and remove it in sections.

5 Backstitch the "bangs" to the head, along the stitch line. Start at the back of the neck and work in a spiral toward the center of the head. For curly hair, leave the loops. For straight hair, cut them off.

Alternative doll faces

You can vary the type of face you give to your dolls by making them with a flat face or by painting instead of embroidering the features.

Flat face

The front head pattern provided on page 14 has a half-seam, which gives the doll a slightly shaped nose. If you prefer a flat face, you can make a new front head pattern by tracing the outline of the front face after the nose seam has been stitched. Cut out in fabric, create features, and stitch to the back head as for the shaped face. See pages 18 and 22.

Painted face

The kit contains thread to embroider the doll's face. However, you can choose to paint or draw the features instead. This method can be used equally successfully for dolls with shaped or flat faces. Embroidery is done after the head is stuffed; painting is best carried out flat on the front head piece, before stitching.

You will need:

Acrylic or fabric paints
• Brown, red, white and black; plus blue if you want blue eyes.
Two fine paintbrushes
• Size 1 or 2.
Small plate or piece of foil
• For use as a palette to mix colors.
Fine permanent ink fabric pen or waterproof drawing pen
• Brown or black.

1 Follow the instructions on page 16 for marking the features on the wrong side of the face fabric. Place the face, right side uppermost, with the drawn features facing downwards onto a piece of white paper. This should allow you to see the features through the fabric.

2 Working on the right side, trace the pencil lines seen through the fabric using a brown or black pen.

3 Mix some brown (or blue) paint with white to lighten it, and paint the iris.

4 Mix red and white paint to make pink. Add a touch of brown if you want a peachy pink. Paint the lips.

5 When the irises are quite dry, paint a large black dot in the center for the pupils.

6 When the pupils are dry, paint a white dot in the top right hand corner of each iris, just touching the pupil, to create highlights.

7 When all the paint is dry, reinforce the lines around the eyelids, eyebrows and between the lips with the pen. Leave to dry thoroughly.

Joining the limbs

Making movable joints

The dollmaking instructions on pages 20–21 explain how to make a doll with limbs stitched to the body. These joints are strong and are suitable for small children. However, a teenager or adult may like to have a doll that can adopt a number of different poses. This can be achieved by jointing the doll with buttons secured by strong thread. Follow the instructions on this page in place of the equivalent stages described on pages 20–21.

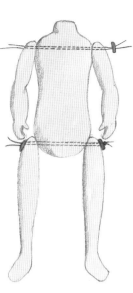

1 Stuff the arms firmly to the top. Turn in the top of each arm and stitch closed as described on page 21.

2 Stuff the legs firmly to the top. Turn in the top of each leg, seam to seam, and shape them in the same way as the arms. Stitch closed with ladder stitch.

3 Stuff the body firmly all the way down and close the bottom section following the rounded shape of the pattern. Ignore the "attach legs here" line shown on the pattern.

4 Thread the large needle with a 1-yard length of doubled strong thread. Thread through one leg, the body, and the second leg. Cut off the thread near the needle, leaving long tails on each side.

5 Thread the two tails on each side through two holes in a button. Tie a knot on each side to hold the buttons in place. Pull the threads and adjust the knots until the joints feel firm and the legs don't swing too loosely. Knot tightly twice more over the buttons. Hide the tails of the threads by twisting them under the button and knotting twice again. Cut off the loose ends.

6 Repeat the procedure with the arms.

You will need:

Four ½in buttons
• In a color that matches the body. Two holes are sufficient. If your buttons have four holes, use two diagonally opposed holes when threading the joint.
Strong thread
• Carpet or linen thread is ideal, but extra-strong sewing thread (buttonhole twist) will do.
Long toy needle or fine darning needle
• This should be at least 3½in long.

The following items are supplied in your Rag Doll kit:

Body
• 21 x 21in unbleached muslin or strong cotton

Filling
• 4oz polyester

Face
• Double-strand embroidery thread:
39in light brown for eyes
39in dark brown for eyebrows, etc.
39in pink for mouth
19¹/2in black for pupils
19¹/2in white for highlights

Hair
• 1oz brown acrylic thick knitting yarn

Making your doll

Everything you need to make a charming traditional rag doll is included in your kit. Just follow the instructions and watch her take shape!

Preparing the pattern

Trace or photo-copy the patterns shown. Make an extra copy of the leg and of the arm. Cut out the patterns following the outlines. In addition, cut out the darts in the paper front head pattern, so that you can mark them more easily. For accuracy and ease of stitching, most patterns *do not* have seam allowances included; the pattern outlines are the sewing lines. The exceptions are the side seams of both the front and back head patterns. These are clearly marked. Follow the instructions carefully and add seam allowances only when instructed.

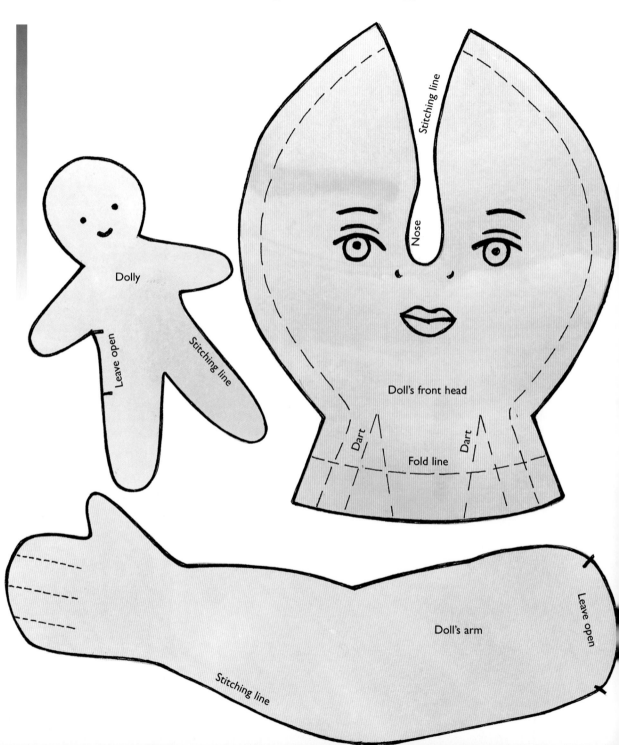

Dolly

Leave open

Stitching line

Stitching line

Nose

Doll's front head

Dart

Dart

Fold line

Doll's arm

Leave open

Stitching line

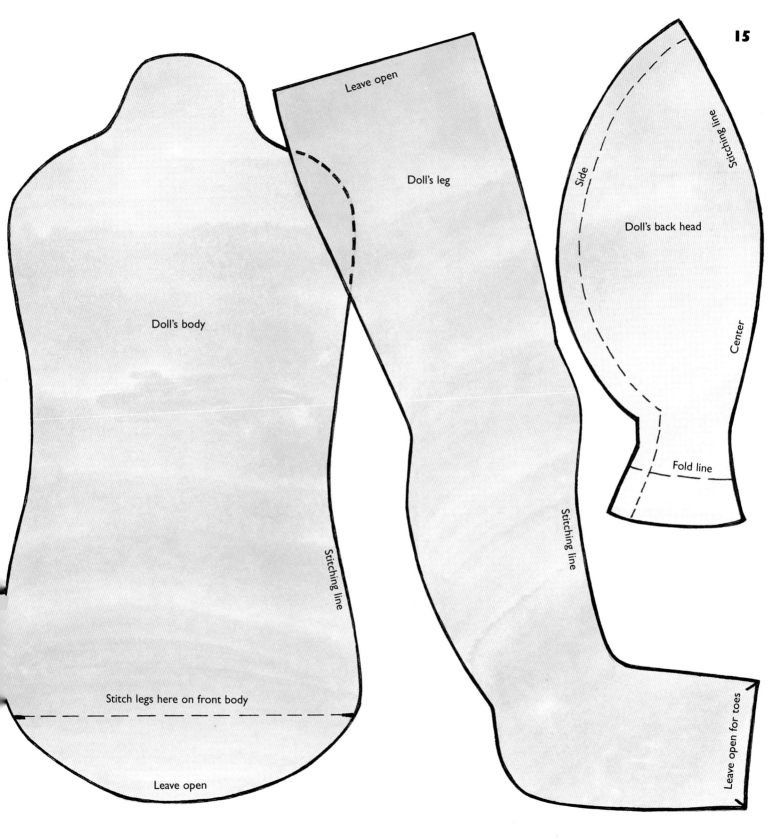

15

Doll's body

Stitch legs here on front body

Leave open

Leave open

Doll's leg

Stitching line

Stitching line

Leave open for toes

Doll's back head

Side

Stitching line

Center

Fold line

Marking the fabric

Before pinning on the patterns, fold the piece of fabric in half. Apart from the head, no pieces should be cut yet.

❤ **1** Place the paper patterns on the fabric as shown. Allow sufficient space between the pieces for seam allowances to be added.

❤ **2** Draw around each pattern piece. Mark the dart in the front head.

❤ **3** Cut around the outside lines of the front head piece only. Open up the folded piece, and place the paper pattern face marked side down. Line up the two and secure with masking tape.

❤ **4** Hold the pattern and fabric up to a window with good light. Trace the features and darts onto the back (wrong side) of the fabric with a soft pencil. The pencil lines should be strong enough to be seen from the right side.

Stitching the fabric

For ease of handling, the pattern pieces are stitched before the fabric is cut. Some seams should have openings. Check the instructions before stitching.

Back head
Stitch center seam only.

1 Fold the face in half, right sides together, and secure with a couple of pins. Stitch the nose seam. Trim the allowance to ⅛in.

Dolly
Leave an opening on one side, as shown.

2 Pin the rest of the doubled fabric together between the marked patterns. Machine stitch around the marked lines, as follows:

Arms
Leave tops open.

Body
Leave lower side open.

Legs
Leave toes and tops open.

Cutting out the pieces

After stitching, cut out the individual pieces with sharp scissors. A seam allowance is added at this stage.

♥ **1** Cut out all the pieces, adding a ¼in seam allowance to every stitched seam and to each traced line (except to the side seams of the front and back head, as explained on page 14). Do *not* cut the darts. Trim the seam allowance to ⅛in around the thumb and hand.

♥ **2** Snip into the curves in the seam allowances – particularly between the thumbs and hands, legs and feet, neck and body, behind the knees, in front of the elbows, and in the back of the neck. Make sure you do not cut into the stitched seams.

The head and toes

1 Open up the seams in the front and back of the head and press open with your fingers. Place the front and back heads right sides together, matching the seams at the top of the head, and at the sides and neck. Pin in place.

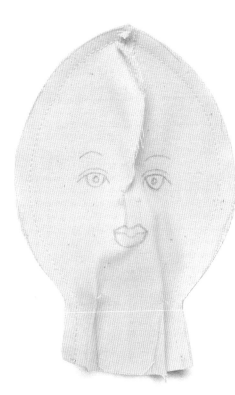

2 Starting at one side of the neck, stitch all around the head, leaving a ¼in seam allowance. Leave the lower part of the neck open.

3 Fold and pin the two darts, and machine or hand stitch. Snip into the curve in the seam allowance between the head and neck.

The head and toes require more detailed stitching than the other parts of the body. You may find it easier to sew some of these pieces by hand.

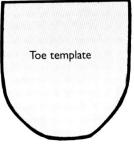

Toe template

4 Trace the toe template onto a piece of paper and cut out.

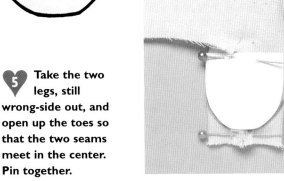

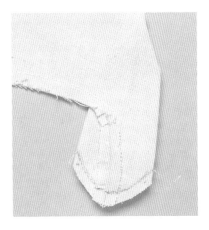

6 Place the toe template on one foot, with the curved side touching the center of the traced toe line. Mark the curve with a pencil. Repeat for the other foot. Carefully stitch the new toe line. Trim the seam allowance to ⅛in.

5 Take the two legs, still wrong-side out, and open up the toes so that the two seams meet in the center. Pin together.

Turning and stuffing

Turn all the pieces right-side out, including the dolly. Use a piece of thin dowelling or tweezers to help turn out the small pieces, such as the thumbs and the dolly's limbs.

Dolly
After stuffing, close up the side opening with ladder stitch.

💚 **1** Stuff only the following pieces:

Head
Stuff this very firmly, but leave the neck unstuffed.

Arms
Stuff the hands and thumbs flatly, rounding between wrist and elbow. Stop 1in from the top.

Legs
Stuff the feet and ankles firmly but softly at the top. Stop stuffing 1in from the top of the legs.

💚 **2** Baste each leg closed about ½in from the top, matching seams, as shown. Pin the legs to the body front, approximately 1in from the lower edge as marked on the paper pattern for the body.

💚 **3** Baste legs in place and then machine or hand stitch twice for strength. The basting will be hidden by the next seam.

💚 **4** Stuff the body ensuring the neck and shoulders are firmly filled.

💚 **5** Bring the back part of the body forward toward the legs. Turn the edge in, and pin. By hand, firmly hem stitch the back body to the legs. Go over the seam twice. Add stuffing to the bottom, if necessary.

Attaching the arms

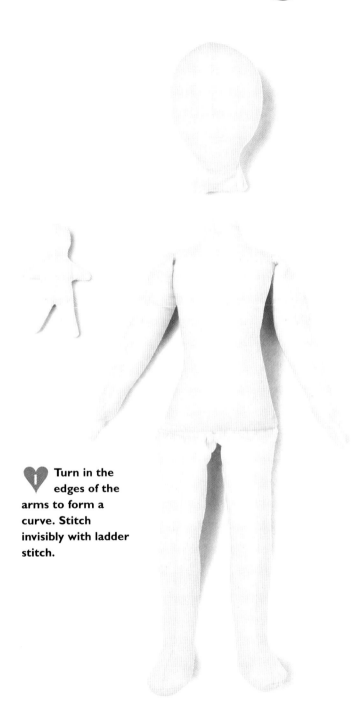

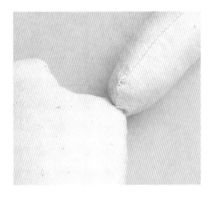

Be sure that the left and right arms are attached to the correct sides of the body and that the thumbs are facing the right way before stitching on the arms.

1 Turn in the edges of the arms to form a curve. Stitch invisibly with ladder stitch.

2 Pin the arms to the shoulders. Join them to the body by ladder stitching only the top ⅜in of the arms' curved edge to the shoulder. Stitch first from the top of the arm, then lift the arm and repeat underneath. Go over the stitching a second time for a strong join.

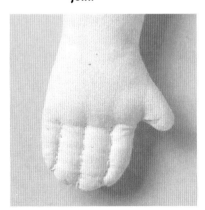

3 Mark the fingers on the back of the hand with pins or pencil dots. Stab stitch between the fingers using double thread. Pull the thread as you work to indent the finger separations.

The face and head

The embroidery thread supplied in the kit is double-stranded. Where instructions specify that you use the thread singly, divide the thread into single strands.

♥ **1** Turn up the neck edge of the doll's head by ½in and baste in place.

💜 **2** The features you marked on the reverse side of the face should be sufficiently visible to serve as a guide for embroidering the features as follows:

Mouth
• Satin stitch the mouth, using the pink thread. Start with the upper lip and continue with the lower lip.

• Using the light brown thread, singly, stem stitch the parting line of the lips. Then do a couple of short stitches for each side of the nose.

Eyes
• Satin stitch the irises with light brown thread.

• Using the dark brown thread, doubled, stem stitch the "eyelashes" along the top of the eyes and the eyebrows (not too far above the eyes).

• Satin stitch the pupil in the center of each eye with black thread.

• Embroider a little highlight with single white thread on the edge of each pupil.

• Using the pink thread, singly, sew a small line of stem stitch ⅟₁₆in above the eye to indicate the eyelid fold.

The Dolly's face
• Using single thread, satin stitch two dark brown dots for the eyes, and stem stitch the line of the mouth.

Alternatively, the face can be painted (see page 10).

💜 **3** Fit the head over the neck on the body. Pin the neck edge to the body, making sure that it is well stretched onto the body so that the head is not wobbly. If necessary, add more stuffing through a small opening. Hand sew the head to the body invisibly with ladder stitch. Remove basting from the neck.

Attaching the hair

The Doll's hair

1 Wind up strands of yarn in two sections, as follows:

• For the main section of hair, with center parting, 18in-long strands, to a width of 3½in.

• For the bangs and back, 12in-long strands, to a width of 2¼in.

Although the hair-making procedure is explained here, the logical point in the sequence, it is recom- mended that the hair is *not* stitched onto the head until *after* the clothes are made. Refer to page 8 for instructions on assembling yarn to make hair.

2 Stitch the bangs and back section onto paper at a distance of 2in from one end. Tear off the paper. Place the stitched line parallel to the seam line on top of the head so that the short section of yarn falls towards the front. Backstitch the yarn onto the head along the stitched line. Pull the back section straight and backstitch to the head about 3in from the top.

3 Stitch the main section of hair onto paper in the middle of the wound yarn, to make a center parting. Tear off the paper and place the yarn so that the parting runs from front to back on the head and so that the yarn falls evenly on each side. Make sure that the front edge of the yarn covers the stitching of the bangs section. Backstitch to the head along the center parting.

4 Cut the loops at the sides and back and comb with your fingers. Trim. Secure the sides of the hair to the doll's head with a few stitches.

Dolly's hair

1 Wind up a few strands of yarn 3½in long. Stitch onto scrap paper along the center line, to make a center parting to a width of 1¼in.

2 Tear off the paper and back- stitch to the dolly's head along the center parting. Cut the loops. Hand stitch to neck and sides.

Making your doll's clothes

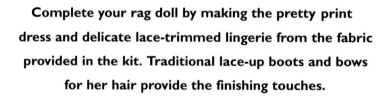

Complete your rag doll by making the pretty print
dress and delicate lace-trimmed lingerie from the fabric
provided in the kit. Traditional lace-up boots and bows
for her hair provide the finishing touches.

Lace-trimmed lingerie

Matching
pantaloons and
petticoat are
essential items
for a traditional
rag doll. The lace
trim provides a
delightfully
delicate finish.

The following
items are
supplied in your
Rag Doll kit:
• 8 x 42in white
fine cotton
polyester
• 36in white lace
edging, ¾in wide
• 15in narrow white
elastic

Pantaloons

1 Trace the
pattern for the
pantaloons twice.
Cut out one
pattern, following
the red lines for the
front. Cut out the
other, following the
black lines for the
back. Join the two
pieces along the side
line with adhesive
tape to make one
whole pattern.

2 Fold one end
of the fabric
so that the pattern
will fit onto doubled
fabric. Pin the
pattern in place and
mark around it. Cut
out. Keep the rest of
the fabric for the
petticoat.

3 Pin the two pieces from waist to crotch
to make two seams along the center
front and the center back. Stitch, leaving a ¼in
seam allowance. Snip curves and press seams
open.

Pantaloons

Front and back

Side – join two halves here

4 Turn up and press ¼in on the lower edge of each leg toward the wrong side. Stitch a piece of lace to the inside edge of each leg.

5 Open up the pantaloons so that front and back seams match. Pin and stitch the underleg seam. Snip curves and finger-press seams open.

6 Turn the waist edge twice to the wrong side, first ¼in and then ⅜in to form a casing. Press, pin, and stitch in place. Leave an opening at the back to slip the elastic through.

Petticoat

1 From the remaining piece of white fabric, mark and cut out a rectangle 8 x 20in.

2 Turn up and fold ¼in along one long edge of fabric and stitch the remaining piece of lace to it to create the petticoat hem. Fold the fabric, right sides together, matching the two short sides. Pin and stitch together. Press seam open.

3 Make a casing on the other long edge by folding it over twice as for the pantaloons. Leave an opening for the elastic.

4 Cut a length of elastic to fit the doll's waist and thread into the casing. Stitch the ends securely together. Turn right side out and adjust gathers.

7 Cut a length of elastic to fit the doll's waist. Thread through the casing and stitch the ends together securely. Adjust waist gathers. Turn right-side out.

Dress pattern pieces

Many of the pattern pieces for the dress are rectangles, the sizes of which are given in Step 2. Make the patterns from plain paper or thin cardboard for accurate marking and cutting of the fabric.

The following items are supplied in your Rag Doll kit:
• 15 x 42in cotton polyester print
• 3 plastic press studs

Note: The fabric supplied should be pressed with a cool iron.

1 Prepare the pattern pieces in paper or cardboard as follows:

Front bodice: Trace the diagram and make two paper or cardboard patterns of the shape. Turn one piece over and join the two pattern pieces along the center front.

Back bodice: Trace the diagram and make two separate pattern pieces. Do not join them.

Sleeves: Make four pattern pieces from the diagram. Turn two of the pieces over and join them in pairs along the middle seam to form two complete sleeve patterns.

Dolly's dress: Make two pattern pieces from the diagram. Turn one piece over and join it to the other.

2 Make rectangular paper patterns according to the dimensions given below. If necessary, join sheets of paper together with adhesive tape for the larger pieces.

Skirt
23½ x 6in

Skirt frill
35 x 3½in

Cuffs (x2)
4½ x 3¼in

Collar
6½ x 2in

Bow
10 x 5in

Center of the bow
2¾ x 4¼in

Pocket
5 x 3¼in

Dolly's bow
5 x 1½in

Center of Dolly's bow
2 x 1½in

Gathering lines

Middle of sleeve – join two halves here

Dress sleeve

Gathering lines

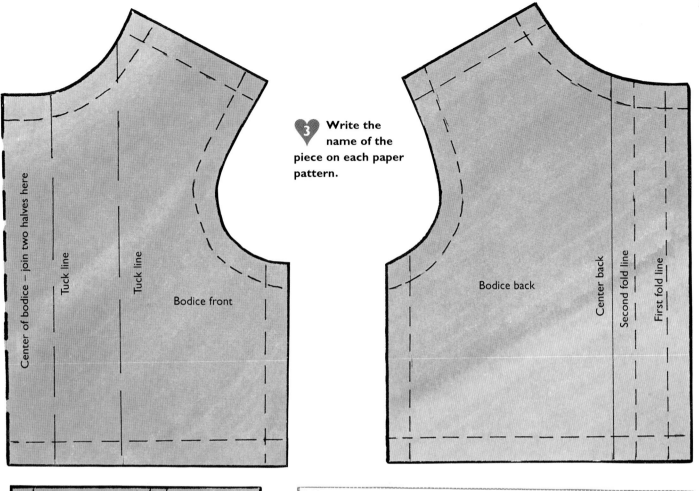

Center of bodice – join two halves here

Tuck line

Tuck line

Bodice front

Bodice back

Center back

Second fold line

First fold line

3 Write the name of the piece on each paper pattern.

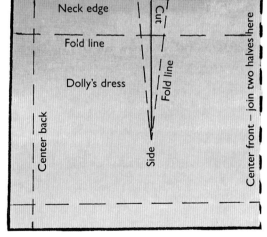

Neck edge

Cut

Fold line

Fold line

Dolly's dress

Center back

Side

Center front – join two halves here

4 Lay all the pattern pieces on the wrong side of the fabric, following the layout. Leave about ¼in on the short edges to allow for the selvages to be trimmed. Mark around all the pieces on the wrong side of the fabric.

5 Cut out the fabric pieces. As soon as each piece is cut, pin a label with its name to it.

Making the bodice

The dress is made in two parts: the bodice and skirt. The bodice has an attractive tucked front, puffed sleeves, and long cuffs.

2   Working on the right side of the front bodice, fold the fabric along the four tuck lines, one at a time. Pin and stitch each tuck ⅛in from the edge of the fold. Press the tucks on each side towards the center.

1   Draw the tuck lines marked on the pattern on the wrong side of the front bodice.

3   Right sides together, pin and stitch the bodice backs to the bodice front at the shoulders only. Press open the seams.

4   Run two rows of gathering stitches along the top edges of the sleeves. Run another two rows of gathering stitches along the bottom edges of the sleeves.

♥ **5** Pull the gathers on the sleeve tops, and adjust to the size of the armholes. Open up the bodice, right-side out and, with right sides together, pin the sleeves into each armhole. Stitch in place and snip curves. Press.

♥ **6** Gather the cuff ends of the sleeves to the length of the shorter edge of the cuff pieces. Right sides together, pin and stitch each cuff piece along a short edge to each sleeve. Press.

♥ **7** Right sides together, stitch the bodice backs to the bodice front along the two underarm seams from the waist to the end of the cuffs. Snip into the underarm curves. Press seams open.

♥ **8** Turn back each cuff edge by ¼in and press. Fold each cuff back up to the seam to conceal the gathered edge. Hand hem to the edge of the sleeve.

♥ **9** Turn in and press ¼in of the back edges of the bodice, but do not stitch yet.

Making the skirt

The dress skirt has a gathered waist and a ruffled hem. A pocket on the skirt front provides the ideal place to keep the little dolly.

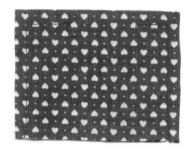

♥ To make the pocket, fold the fabric piece in half lengthwise, right sides together. Stitch the raw edges together, leaving a gap in the middle side. Trim the corners and turn right side out. Press and ladder stitch the gap closed.

2 To make the skirt hem, turn up one long edge of the skirt frill by ¼in. Then turn it again by ⅜in. Press and stitch in place. Run two rows of gathering stitches along the other long edge.

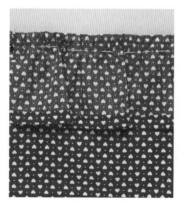

3 Pull ruffle gathers evenly to fit the long edge of the skirt piece. Right sides together, pin and stitch it to one of the long edges of the skirt piece. Press seam to one side only. Run two rows of gathering stitches along the top edge of the skirt piece. Place pins to mark the center and quarter points of the skirt waist. Pull the skirt gathers to fit the lower edge of the bodice.

Making up the dress

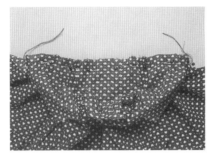

1 **Right sides together, pin skirt and bodice together. Stitch and press seam to one side.**

Pin the bodice and skirt together, matching the center points. The quarter points pinned in the skirt should align with the side seams of the bodice.

2 **With the folded edge uppermost, pin the pocket to the skirt, 2in down from the waist, and 1¼in to the right side of the center of the skirt. Stitch it to skirt along the sides and bottom.**

3 **Right sides together, pin and stitch the back seam of the skirt up to 2½in from the waist. Press seam open. Turn in the edges, following the line of the seam, press and stitch in place.**

4 **Turn dress right side out. Pin and stitch one long end of the collar to the neck edge. Fold in the short ends, and fold the collar lengthwise twice. Hand hem onto the inside of the neck.**

5 **Stitch one snap on the collar, one on the waist, and one halfway between the previous two.**

Bows

Bows made from the same fabric as the dress, attached to the hair of both the doll and dolly, provide a neat finish for the back of the head. Fold both lengths of fabric in half widthwise, right sides together, before you start.

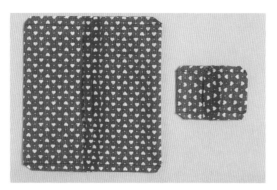

1 For each bow, stitch the long edge opposite the fold, leaving an opening in the middle. Press seam open.

2 Open up the piece so that the seam is in the middle. Stitch across the top and bottom and trim the corners.

3 Turn right side out. Push the corners out with a blunt tip, such as the handle of a small paintbrush. Press flat.

4 For the centers of the bows, fold fabric pieces in half lengthwise, right sides together. Stitch the edge opposite the fold, leaving a ¼in seam allowance. Turn right-side out, leaving the short edges raw – they will be hidden later.

5 Run a gathering stitch along the middle of each bow along the center seam. Pull to gather. Wrap the corresponding center piece around the gathered center, folding the raw edges to the back. Stitch in place. Attach the bows to the back of the doll and dolly heads after the hair has been attached.

Boots

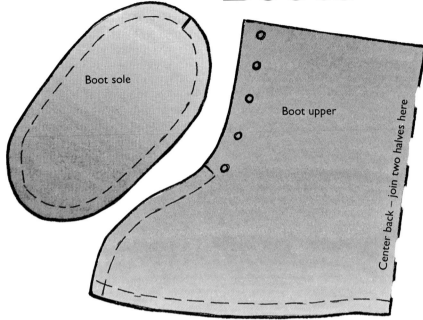

Boot sole

Boot upper

Center back – join two halves here

1 Place the two complete patterns for the boot uppers and the two sole patterns on the wrong side of the boot fabric.

2 Mark the patterns on the fabric with a ballpoint pen and cut out the pieces.

Make four paper patterns of the boot upper, and two of the sole pattern. Join the boot upper patterns back to back in pairs.

The following items are supplied in your Rag Doll kit:
- 15¾ x 3⅛in imitation suede
- 39in fine cord

3 Fold each boot right sides together and stitch from the sole end to point A on the pattern.

4 Still wrong-side out, pin, baste, and then stitch each sole to each boot.

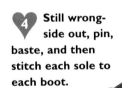

5 Turn the boots right-side out. Make five little holes for the laces in the places indicated in the pattern. Thread the laces. Put the boots on the doll and finish each one with a bow.

Dolly's dress

1 Fold, press, and hem all edges of the dress as shown, starting with the underarms and finishing with the neck, which has a slightly wider hem.

2 Run a gathering stitch along the neck edge, ⅛in down from the folded edge. Fit the dress on the dolly and stitch it closed at the back.

Accessories

You can easily make an entire wardrobe of clothes
for your rag doll. The dress pattern can be used
with a warm fabric to make a winter dress.
Complete the outfit with a hat, cape, and pouch.

Cape

Keep your doll warm in cold weather with a beautiful velvet cape trimmed in fur fabric. Make it in a color that coordinates with the hat.

You will need:
Crushed velvet
• 18 x 25in
Ribbon
• 30in x ½in in a matching or contrasting color
Fur fabric
• 36 x 1½in

1 Make a paper pattern by enlarging the template to twice the size (200 percent). Fold the fabric in half, right sides together, and place the pattern with the center back edge on the fold. Pin in place and cut out. From the remaining fabric, cut a collar band, 12in by 4in.

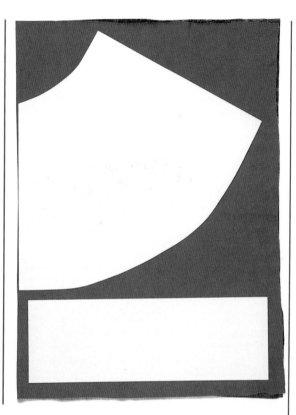

3 Fold the band lengthwise to the wrong side, to make a collar width of 1in. Pin along the seam. On the inside of the collar, fold the edge of the remaining fabric inward to make a ½in casing. Pin in place. Stitch along the cape/collar seam. Then stitch along the folded edge of the casing. Leave the ends of the casing open.

2 Right sides together, pin one long edge of the collar band to the neck edge of the cape so that the ends of the band extend evenly beyond the edges of the cape on each side. Stitch a ⅜in seam. Trim the ends of the band to ½in. Fold the ends of the bands inward so that they are flush with the edge of the cape. Hem by hand or machine.

4 Cut the strip of fur fabric in half lengthwise. Cut two 10in lengths from one of the strips, and pin each to one of the two front raw edges of the cape, starting just below the casing. Hand hem in place along both edges of each fur

strip. Trim the ends, if necessary. Pin and stitch the remaining fur strip to the lower edge of the cape in the same way.

Center back – place on fold

Neck

Cape

Trim with fur

Center front

Trim with fur

Half-size pattern

5 Thread the ribbon through the casing. Put the cape on the doll and pull the ribbon to gather the neck edge. Finish with a bow.

Hat

A lovely wide-brimmed hat provides a stylish finish to your rag doll's winter outfit.

You will need:

Felt
• 15 x 7½in
Ribbon
• 24in x ½in in a contrasting color

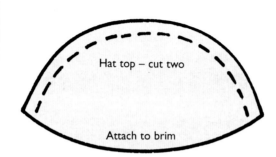

Hat top – cut two

Attach to brim

Snip

Attach to hat top

Hat brim

Half-size patterns

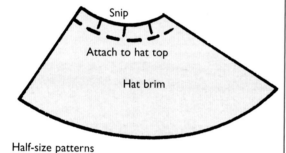

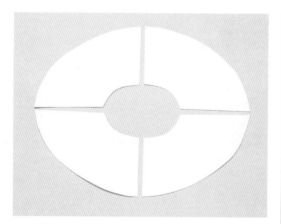

1 Make paper patterns by enlarging the templates to twice the size (200 percent) and cut out. Draw around the brim piece four times onto a sheet of paper. Turn the paper pattern over and around as necessary to make a complete oval-shaped brim pattern. Cut out the pattern carefully.

2 Place the brim piece onto the felt and draw around the pattern. Cut it out just inside the outline. Carefully cut out the center section. Snip the inner edge at ½in intervals, to a depth of ¼in.

3 Cut out two hat top pieces from the felt. Place the pieces right sides together, pin and stitch a ¼in seam along the longer curved edge. Turn right-side out and match to the inner edge of the brim. Pin in place with the brim edge inside. Hand or machine stitch close to the edge.

4 Cut a 12in piece of ribbon and pin along the edge of the top, starting at one side seam. Stitch in place along both long edges. Fold one end over the other, overlap and stitch in place. Make a bow with long tails with the remaining ribbon. Attach it to the hat, covering the ribbon overlap.

Pouch

Half-size pattern

Pouch base

Leave open

💜 1 Make a paper pattern of the pouch base by enlarging the template to twice the size (200 percent). Cut a rectangle of fabric 4½in by 8in. Fold the remaining fabric in half, and outline the oval pattern in the center. Mark a 6mm ¼in seam allowance around the oval. Pin the layers of fabric together and stitch along the inner line, leaving an opening on one side as indicated. Cut out the oval shape following the outer line of the seam allowance. Turn right-side out and close the opening with ladder stitch.

💜 2 Right sides together, fold the fabric rectangle in half. Pin the short sides together and stitch ¼in from the edge. Make a casing along one raw edge by folding first ¼in and then ½in to the wrong side. Pin in place and stitch near the edge, leaving an opening for the ribbon.

💜 3 Run a gathering stitch along the other edge. Turn right side out. Pull gathers slightly, leaving a hole slightly smaller than the oval piece. Right sides together, pin the oval onto the gathered edges. Hand hem in place.

💜 4 Thread the ribbon through the casing, and tie the ends together about 1in from the ends.

This can be made in the same fabric as that of the cape, or in red cotton to match the kit dress.

You will need:

Fabric
• 11 x 5in
Ribbon
• 20in x ½in

Nightgown

Your doll may need something to wear for sleeping, so here is a delicate nightie for her to put on at night.

You will need:
• 42 x 18in fine cotton or cotton polyester
• 7in thin elastic

1 Make two copies of the pattern, enlarged to twice the size (200 per cent). Cut out one along the center back line, and the other along the center front line. Fold the fabric right sides together. Place the front piece with its center line along the fold and cut it out. Place the back piece on the remaining doubled fabric and cut out two backs. Cut a fabric strip 22in by 1½in.

2 With the two backs right sides together, pin and stitch center back seam from A to B. Press seams open.

3 Right sides together, place the front and back against each other. Pin the shoulders together and stitch in place. Press seams open.

4 Turn the nightgown right side out. Run a gathering row ¼in from the neck edge, and gather to obtain a neck circumference of 6in.

5 Right sides together, match the center of the fabric strip to the center front of the neckline. Pin and stitch around neck, leaving a ¼in seam allowance. Press outward. Fold strip lengthwise twice and pin in place on inside of neck. Stitch in place. Turn short edges in to make neat.

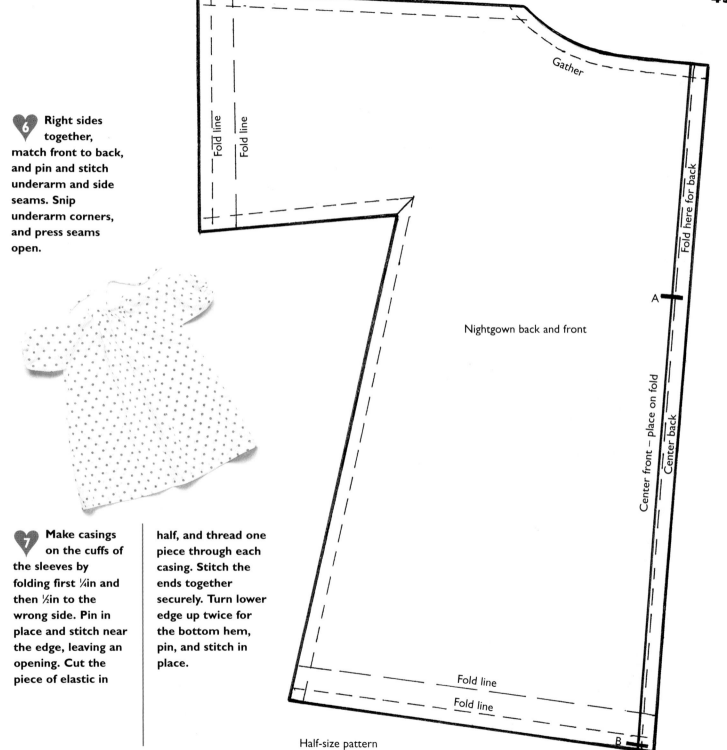

6 **Right sides together,** match front to back, and pin and stitch underarm and side seams. Snip underarm corners, and press seams open.

7 **Make casings on the cuffs of** the sleeves by folding first ¼in and then ½in to the wrong side. Pin in place and stitch near the edge, leaving an opening. Cut the piece of elastic in half, and thread one piece through each casing. Stitch the ends together securely. Turn lower edge up twice for the bottom hem, pin, and stitch in place.

Fold line

Fold line

Gather

Fold here for back

A

Nightgown back and front

Center front – place on fold

Center back

Fold line

Fold line

B

Half-size pattern

Hello Dolly

Rag dolls come in an array of types and sizes from traditional rag dolls with brightly colored hair to starker Shaker-style dolls with fabric scrap hair and minimal features.

On the following pages, a selection of rag dolls in an exciting variety of styles are pictured.

Once you have made your first rag doll, use these styles for inspiration in future doll-making projects.

Whether your preference is for pretty girl dolls in ruffles and floral prints, or for exotic dolls in authentic ethnic dress, there are styles of rag doll to suit every taste. All the dolls shown here have stuffed fabric bodies and simple sewn or painted faces.

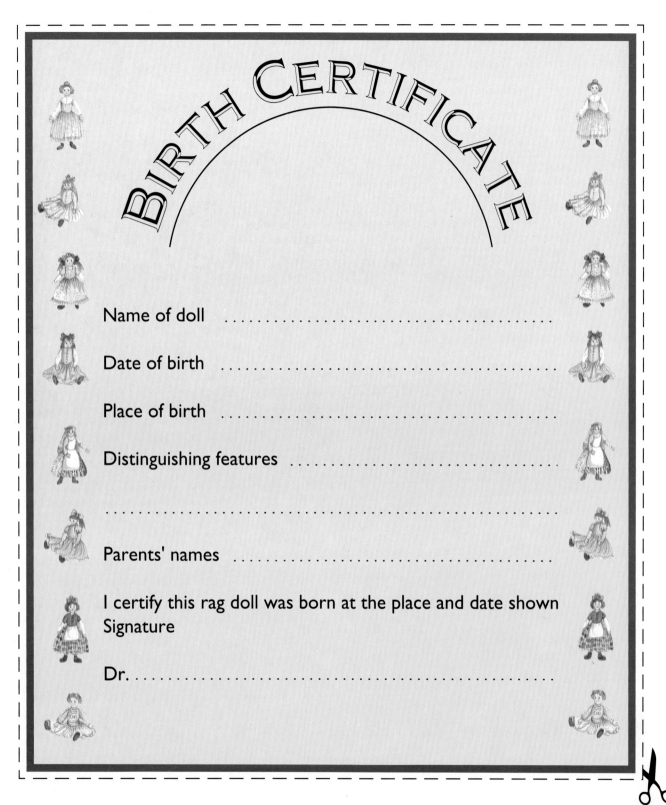

BIRTH CERTIFICATE

Name of doll ....

Date of birth ....

Place of birth ....

Distinguishing features ....

....

Parents' names ....

I certify this rag doll was born at the place and date shown
Signature

Dr. ....